Setting Goals, Getting Goals

Achieve Your Full Potential Through Goal Setting, Planning And Time Management

Table of Contents

Introduction

I want to thank you and congratulate you for purchasing this book, "Setting Goals, Getting Goals: *Achieve Your Full Potential Through Goal Setting, Planning, And Time Management.*"

This book contains proven steps and strategies about how to set and implement effective goals and how to utilize time management techniques.

With the help of this book, one can have a thorough understanding of goal setting as a concept, theory and as an act. This book recognizes the significance of a full comprehension of how goal-setting works and how exactly it is done. This book will help you understand why some people fail in achieving their goals while others seem to not even break a sweat in attaining their desired outcomes. This book offers a guide on how one can make effective goals that are likely to be achieved.

Also, this book talks about time management. Time is a very important resource; however, it is a limited kind. The complexity of life particularly nowadays makes it necessary for people to learn the habit of time management. Fortunately, specific guidelines on how to build an effective time management system that would allow you to live a happy and fulfilled life are found in the pages of this book.

Chapter 1: Introduction To Goal Setting And Planning

Human beings are goal-oriented by nature. The processes related to goals and goal setting helps an individual develop motivation, organization and direction for his or her behaviors. With goals, an individual is provided with ideal outcomes and standards that are worthy of consideration. These will help a person evaluate his or her own functioning in relation to the different aspects or domains of life.

A person may aim at different things throughout his or her lifespan. His or her goals may be framed in varying ways. It is possible for one to have goals hinged at promoting some positive results or avoiding negative outcomes. Goals could also be framed as an attempt to demonstrate competence or to acquire competence. Life goals could also be based on an intrinsic or extrinsic reward. Although these framings can definitely influence the success of one's goal attainment, there are other factors that must also be given adequate attention.

For instance, a person's goal may remain dormant for years if there is no sufficient commitment pushing a person to pursue it. Indeed, a sense of commitment is one major factor that could positively or negatively impact the attainment of one's goals. Setting a goal which one can strongly commit to will be very useful in life. It is also revealed in studies that goals backed up with strong commitments have higher chances of being achieved.

A person's commitment to a certain goal is largely influenced by the perceived desirability and feasibility of the said objectives. Desirability refers to the overall belief of the person regarding the pleasantness of the expected consequences of goals. Feasibility, on the other hand, is the expectations that something, an event or an outcome, is likely to occur. Nevertheless, experts believe that a desirable goal with high feasibility cannot guarantee a strong goal commitment just yet.

What are Goals? What are Plans?

It is necessary for one to understand the concepts underlying goal setting and planning to be able to fully comprehend these processes. Hence, it is deemed necessary to elaborate on term definition in this section.

Goals pertain to mental representations of desired future outcomes to which people attach certain level of commitment. By setting goals, one recognizes the discrepancy between the desired state and the current state. This discrepancy is a hindrance in achieving the desired outcome; hence, one is aimed at working on reducing it. It is, however, possible for one to consider desirable future states without committing to them. Only when one is willing to exert effort and invest affect, behavior and cognition to reach the desired state is he or she dedicated to goal attainment.

Whilst the goal intention identifies a desired state, it is the goal commitment that describes how much the outcome is desired. Consequently, having just the intention to set goals is insufficient.

In simple terms, goals are the desired state of an organization or a person in the future. It is the goal that states the purpose of an individual or group; hence, it undeniably plays a pivotal role. For one to be able to achieve these goals, specific steps or measures must be followed. Such a blueprint for achieving the goal is called the *plan*. Aside from the specific actions and tasks, plans involve schedules and resource allocation. Putting and elaborating these two concepts together describes the concept of planning. Indeed, planning incorporates defining one's goals and determining the means by which they will be realized.

In the corporate world, what lies on top of the goals hierarchy is the mission. In a business milieu, mission states the general reason why an organization is in existence. It summarizes in a broad manner the aspirations, reasons for being and values of the company. The mission is significant as the subsequent, specific goals are based on it. Hence, if the mission of an organization or even of a single individual is unclear, the goals together with the plans may be developed randomly, steering the person or a group in the wrong direction.

Just like a mission, strategic goals are broad statements stating where the person or an organization wants to be in the future. Going hand-in-hand with strategic goals are strategic plans. These are the specific steps, actions and resources needed to achieve the strategic goal.

A more elaborate statement of goals is called tactical goals. In the corporate world, tactical goals refer to the specific goals assigned to different departments of the organization. Tactical plan is the term used to describe the accompanying steps of execution to achieve the goals of every department. On a personal level, a person's plan for the different aspects of his or her life can be likened to the tactical goals of the corporate world.

Finally the most specific type of goals is called operational goals. This is the highly particular set of goals given to every individual in a corporation to achieve. On a personal level, these goals are the specific everyday objectives a person is aiming at.

Goals and plans always go together. Without any plan of action, a person or an organization will find it difficult to reach their objectives. In the same manner, a plan is useless if the end goal is missing or unclear.

Chapter 2: Theories Behind Goal, Goal Setting And Goal Implementation

Goal-Setting Theory

With nearly 400 studies concentrating on goals, pioneers Edwin Locke and Gary Latham (1990) came up with the goal-setting theory and task performance. In said studies, the term 'goal' was defined as that which an individual is trying to accomplish or do. According to this theory, a person's values and intentions are two cognitive determinants of his or her behavior. It is more likely for a person to pursue intentions or goals that are aligned with his or her values. Furthermore, the theory supports the notion that goals can influence behavior or job performance for employees. Locke and Latham strongly believe that a goal, therefore, has the ability to direct a person's actions and attentions.

Today it is acknowledged that goal setting has a pervasive impact on employee performance and behavior in management and organization practices. Consequently, some form of goal setting is present in the operations of almost all modern companies. It is widely accepted to company managers that goal setting is necessary to sustain and improve performance at work.

According to the studies conducted, giving a person general and easy kinds of goal does not make a person produce the desired behavior of better performance and productivity. The same is true when there was no goal set at all. What makes a person do better with tasks is a set of specific, challenging and difficult goals. However, studies also revealed other factors that could influence the effectiveness of goal setting. Such factors include the person's ability plus the way he or she internalize goals and receive feedback on his or her performance.

To make goals effective, goal setting theory states that certain conditions must first be met. Goal acceptance is one of the said conditions. Without acceptance, goals are generally futile. A goal cannot motivate a person who is not at all willing to own the goal and commit to it. Once the goals are personalized, the person has a sufficient and significant reason to exert effort on pursuing the goals.

Following goal acceptance is goal commitment. According to the goal setting theory, there are two factors that influence a person's degree of determination in pursuing goals. One of these is called self-efficacy and the other is importance. Self-efficacy refers to the person's belief that he or she can achieve the goals set. Importance, on the other hand, refers to the factors making the goal achievement and its outcomes significant. Consequently, if the person has owned the goal, which he or she sees as being significant and achievable, then it can be expected that goal commitment and striving will be high.

Furthermore, according to the theory, when a person understands the rationale or purpose of the goal, it is likely that they will be more committed and motivated to pursue it.

Fantasy Realization Theory

Gabriel Oettingen developed a theory that takes into consideration people's readiness to set goals in terms of their free fantasy about their future selves. This theory distinguishes between two ways that people think of their future. One is *free fantasies* and the other is *expectations*. The former refers to the thoughts about the desired future that are not dependent on the likelihood that these thoughts will materialize. The latter, on the other hand, are mental judgments regarding the probability that a certain future event will occur.

Oettingen mentioned three ways that people handle their future free fantasies. One of these is mentally contrasting the positive desired future against the negative aspects of the present reality. Mental contrasting makes the person see the desired future as the one that must be attained, whilst the hindrance posted by the present must be changed.

The second way that people address their future fantasies is indulgence. This makes a person too consumed by the desirable future, making him or her disregard the impending reality. Such thinking makes a person less eager to act, as he or she cannot see the factors of the present that needs to be changed in order to attain the desired outcome.

Dwelling on the negative factors of the present is the third way mentioned by Oettingen. If a person merely dwells in the present negativities, he or she will fail to see the positive rewards of the desired future. Consequently, he or she will not be motivated to act on attaining the future fantasies.

Fantasy realization model posits that people imagine the accomplishment of the desired outcome or future and then consider the reality at hand that is generally standing in the way of the preferred future. Furthermore, this theory suggests that when people contrast the future and the present, they are creating expectancy-dependent commitment on goals. Mental contrasting allows people to assess the feasibility of their goals by simultaneously linking the desired future and the present.

Provided that the expectations for success or the feasibility of the desired outcome is high, people commit strongly to achieving the goal. However, if the feasibility is low, people will either have a very low commitment to attaining the goal or none at all. Therefore, mental contrast guides people in identifying which among their goals are achievable and which are not.

Mental contrasting can help people protect their resources such as time, money and effort. However, there are people who tend to dwell just on the present negativity and others tend to overly indulge themselves in the desired future. Goals set for either kinds of assessment are likely to waste human resources instead of protecting them. The goal commitment of people in one-sided elaborations is moderate but with mental contrasting people are led to making smart goal commitments.

The process making people's vague ideas about their future selves into a smart goal commitment or a half-hearted one is the focus of fantasy realization theory. In one particular study, students who utilized mental contrast earned grades significantly closer to their expectations. Students who had their *success expectations* at a high level were the most energized group. Also, they were the ones who exerted the most effort and they received the highest of the grades. In contrast, students who perceived low feasibility were the least energized; hence, they devoted too little effort in performing the tasks. Consequently, they got the lowest grades.

Several different studies revealed the same pattern as the above-mentioned. With high feasibility, people utilizing mental contrasting showed the strongest commitment to the goals. People with low expectations of success, on the other hand, displayed the least commitment in striving for the goals. Moreover, people who either dwell in the present or indulge excessively in the desirable future displayed moderate commitment and striving, regardless of whether their perceived feasibility is high or low.

Mental contrasting involves looking at and elaborating the desirable future and then assessing the present reality. In such chronology, the future is turned into a focal reference to which the present is compared and contrasted. Changing the order, however, alters the effect of the self-regulation process as well. If the present reality is assessed first before elaborating the desired future, it is likely that the person will not see the present as a hindrance to the desired success. In turn, the commitment to the goal will not be congruent with the success expectation of the person.

Other Related Theories

Several other theories contribute to the current body of knowledge about goals, motivation and goal setting. One of these is called *achievement goal theory*. According to this theory, to demonstrate abilities is the primary intent of people in achievement contexts.

Furthermore, this theory suggests that there are two conceptions of a person's ability that occur in contexts of achieving goals. Such conceptions manifest in the form of goal states called 'ego' and 'task'. According to Nicholls, there are people who consider themselves in a task performance state when in achievement context. These kinds of people believe that by developing skills, exerting maximum effort and increasing their competence level, they can demonstrate their abilities clearly. While task involvement views success as the demonstration of mastery, ego involvement's success is perceived once performance exceeds that of others, especially when little effort was exerted. Indeed, people who are in the state of ego involvement view social comparison as the focal point. In contrast, people who are task oriented are self-referencing.

Self-determination theory offers another perspective that is gaining popularity as well. This theory stands at a multidimensional and need-based approach to fully understand people's affectivity, behavioral and cognitive responses. Self-determination theory claims that people have innate needs for relatedness, autonomy and competence. These basic needs, as according to the theory, must be satisfied by the social or achievement context for performance, motivation and development to be facilitated. This theory also states that there are three motivation types that may influence a person's determination namely, extrinsic motivation, intrinsic motivation and amotivation.

Extrinsic motivation drives a person to perform or participate in order to avoid a punishment or to get an external reward. On the other hand, intrinsic motivation makes a person join or perform an activity for his or her own sake. What motivates him or her is the satisfaction or pleasure received directly from participating in the task or goal. A person's self-determination is high when he or she is intrinsically motivated. The least self-determined construct is the amotivation. This refers to the absence or lack of motivation or intention to perform. This happens when a person does not see the goals as important or if he or she lacks any sense of competence.

Self-determination theory, essentially, points out that the highest self-determination level can be achieved if there is an intrinsic motivation; hence, a positive outcome can be expected. On the contrary, amotivation is believed to lead to negative outcomes.

Another theory used the fundamental tenets of self-determination theory to introduce yet other factors that are deemed necessary in understanding goal setting and motivation. Vallerand suggested that people's motivation operates in three levels. He called these levels 'situational', 'contextual' and 'global'. Situational motivation, according to Vallerand, pertains to the motivation a person experiences while performing a specific task or activity. Contextual motivation refers to the adopted motivation predisposition of a person in specific contexts. For instance, a person is intrinsically motivated at home while amotivated at work. Finally, Vellerland likened global motivation to the personality type of the individual. Consequently, this kind of motivation refers to the general way a person interacts with his or her immediate environment. Vallerand also pointed out that motivation is such a complex notion that must not be understood at a general level.

Goal Implementation

Setting goal intentions requires one to specify that which he or she desires as an outcome. Nevertheless, this is just one of the pre-requisites of goal pursuit. What comes next to setting goal intentions is the initiation of goal-directed behaviors. This can easily be accomplished if the behaviors necessary are routine or well practiced. Unfortunately, most of the time, that is not the case.

To promote behaviors that are goal-directed, Gollwitzer suggested a kind of intention he labeled *implementation intention*. The formula for this self-regulatory strategy is *"I intend to perform/do X once I encounter situation Y."* By using implementation intention, one is anticipating situations in the future and is linking these to a specific goal-directed behavior. According to Gollwitzer, when implementation intention is performed, a person is committing to the goal-oriented behavior to address critical circumstances.

It appears that implementation intention is similar to planning. The two, however, carry significant differences. Implementation intention is simpler than planning. It only involves one specific goal-directed action and one particular situation.

Implementation intention can also be likened to prospective memory. Nevertheless, unlike some memory technique, implementation intention does not need any repeated rehearsal of what to do. It only takes a single will to instigate the goal-oriented behavior from the moment the specified situation took place. Also, implementation intention does not need any mnemonics, both internal and external, to remind the person to perform the goal-oriented behavior. It can be expected that the specified situation will automatically activate the intended behavior.

There are several studies affirming the benefits of implementation intention. Studies show that implementation intention can help promote behaviors that are desired but infrequently performed, objective measures and self-reports and behavioral performance of people from the academe and the general public.

The effectiveness of implementation intention in goal attainment is mainly caused by the automaticity of the goal-directed behaviors. From the moment the specified situation is experienced, the intended behavior appears immediately, even without the full awareness of the person doing the action.

Chapter 3: Functions Of Goal Setting And Planning

Life has a lot of uncertainties. Some people are afraid of the future for it is unknown. The present can be too overwhelming for many. With such distractions, a person or an organization can be headed in different random directions that may or may not result in the desired outcome. Indeed, steering the wheel of life can be difficult if there is no specific destination set.

Having specific goals in life gives a person a sense of direction. Where he or she wants to be in the future will determine the path he or she has to take. One of the major functions served by having goals is the guidance it provides to one's actions. With clear objectives in life, a person can direct his or her attention and efforts to the specific targets necessary to reach the desired future. There is just so much that the world can offer, particularly nowadays; hence, it is important for one to be focused on the things that matter greatly for what he or she desires for the future.

The presence of goals enhances commitment and motivation among people. Goals are like an energy source fueling people to keep on striving even in the face of difficulties. The rewards of the desired future are what motivate people to pursue goals. Its desirability makes it attractive and worthwhile.

People are generally uncomfortable with uncertainties, but with goals, people get a clearer view of what they need to do for a certain period of time. This reduces the ambiguity of life; hence, people become more determined to pursue the clear future outcomes for they know how to get there.

The decision making process also becomes less haphazard and more logical if a person or an organization has clear and specific goals. It is likely that if a person or group is committed to a certain goal, decisions will be aligned to the success of the goal achievement. For instance, a person aiming at getting an A+ grade at the end of the school year will not yield to peer pressure of partying every night. In relation to this, having goals creates a certain standard that assesses the performance or behavior of the person or employees. With a goal in mind and a plan at hand, a person will know how much effort is needed to reach his or her desirable future. One's performance is likely to increase if he or she has strongly committed to the goal set.

Keeping goals also allow an individual or group to wisely utilize resources. For instance, time is a valuable resource for people and it is something one cannot recycle. Hence, it must be managed and used accordingly. If one has no clear goals, he or she is likely to waste time doing things unnecessary to his or her desired outcome. Money is another resource that must be allotted accordingly. To be able to maximize such limited resources, a detailed plan is necessary.

Chapter 4: Why Set Goals?

Goal setting, perhaps, is the most researched topic in the field of industrial psychology. Hundreds of studies support the notion that setting goals can really be beneficial for people. Experimental and correlational studies conducted revealed that by explicitly setting goals a person's performance at any task can significantly improve. Having clear goals in mind, a person is also able to display a better capacity to self-regulate. This is manifested by a person's ability to direct efforts and focus towards activities that are goal-relevant.

According to studies, setting clear goals can also increase enthusiasm among people. This is because more important goals can lead to more production of energy. Also, well-defined goals can make a person more persistent, which in turn makes him or her less vulnerable to disappointments, anxiety and frustration. Also, setting goals clears a person's mind; hence, one has better chances of discovering and utilizing more efficient perception and thought strategies.

In addition to this, a study conducted by Emmons and Deiner revealed that goal attainment is significantly correlated with positive affectivity among undergraduate students. They found out that even the mere presence of significant goals (self-rated) elicits positive affects among student and the correlation is as strong as that of actually achieving the goals. In a separate study, it was discovered that a greater feelings of well-being was a byproduct of perceived progress in goal attainment.

Another recent study on goal setting in the academic milieu revealed the same pattern as the previous research. In comparison with the control group, undergraduates who underwent a complete program on goal setting experienced significant benefits. Those who completed said program were found to have the highest probability of keeping a full load course. Also, they were the ones who made significant increases in their GPAs. Lastly, they experienced less self-reported negative affectivity.

Goal setting was also found to be capable of inspiring people and this is considered pivotal in a person's self-management. Goals also provide challenges to a person, which makes him or her overcome even seemingly exhausting tasks. While being able to perform tasks accordingly and meet the standards set by the specified goals, a person then develops a sense of pride and enhanced self-esteem. Such developments can lead a person to a better and healthier mindset, which in turn will make him or her more productive.

The undeniable popularity and the extensive research conducted supporting goal setting theory are sufficient enough to make most organizations and even individuals consider setting goals a priority. Nevertheless, this does not mean that the theory does not have limitations.

One major limitation of goal setting is called *tunnel vision.* This refers to the possibility that focusing too much on the task narrows one's attention to the point that he or she no longer sees other aspects of the job that are worthy of attention. It is highly probable that too much concentration on the goal will cause one to miss major environmental aspects.

The effectiveness of goal setting in an organizational context can also be challenged by inequity among workers. Also, if the goals are always imposed on people, motivating themselves can be difficult.

Goal setting theory is not without flaws. There are critics emphasizing the limitations of the theory. Nevertheless, the vast amount of research supporting the effectiveness of setting goals cannot be discarded. Consequently, goal setting has remained highly valued by corporations and even by individuals.

Chapter 5: What Makes An Effective Goal?

Some of the limitations of goal setting theory are minor enough that certain adjustments with the way goals are made can readily solve the issue. For instance, a person is aiming at two goals; however, focusing and directing efforts on one goal will result in difficulty achieving the other. By finding a balance between goals or by setting priorities among goals, this particular issue can be solved. Indeed, setting goals is not as easy as wishful thinking and listing them all. Goal setting is a process that must be thought of before planning and implementation. For a goal to be effective, therefore, it has to pass certain criteria that will increase the likelihood of its success.

Before elaborating on the characteristics of effective goals, it is first important to stress that understanding the rationale for the goals' existence is of utmost significance. One must be able to fully grasp why he or she is pursuing something. This way, the person is likely to have stronger commitment and motivation to perform better and attain what is desired.

In setting goals, one needs to be *specific*. This is the very first consideration for one to come up with effective goals. Across varying studies about performance and memory, it was revealed that specific goals are the ones that can raise performance significantly. In several pieces of research, the presence of specific goals was found to create stronger and longer motivational effect on participants.

Vague goals tend to appear overwhelming and unobtainable for people. Generally stated goals do little to motivate people. Hence, it is common to hear others saying, *"I'll definitely change for the better."* Nevertheless, after weeks, months and years, nothing really changes. The problem with this goal is its vagueness. It is most likely that the person who stated such broad objective does not really know where to begin. Worse, he or she does not really understand what the problem is or where the problem is coming from.

Indeed, in identifying goals one must be clear, detailed and informed. Changing for the better is just too amorphous. Why is there a need to change? What needs to be changed? How will one change? There are just several unknown details in such goal; hence, it is not surprising that people with such vague aims do not progress with any kind of change even after a long while.

Nevertheless, one can utilize such general goals to come up with more specific ones. By answering the *who, what, where, when, how* and *why* questions, it is easier for one to reduce the vagueness of his or her goal. As much as the written goals can be further detailed, one must not stop trying to come up with more specific ones. Only when the written goals can no longer be elaborated (as it is already fully detailed) can one say that he or she has specific goals to pursue.

Having vague goals are also a problem for most students. It is common for them to aim at *doing better in school*, which is too broad for a goal. Reducing such general idea into more specific ones like *"Starting tomorrow, I will devote three straight hours to doing school work and nothing else"* or *"My GPA will be increased by 0.7 at the end of this semester"* makes the goal sound more achievable.

Even in an organizational setting, it was revealed by studies that employees perform at significantly higher levels when they are instructed to achieve specific aims. Consequently, a manger who keeps on telling an organization member to *"do your best,"* or *"work hard"* is not helping at all.

Aside from increasing the levels of performance of employees, it was also found that specific goals can reduce turnover, absenteeism and tardiness.

The next criterion for an effective goal is being *measurable*. In setting goals, one must make sure that there is a concrete way of measuring progress in goal attainment. As much as one does not know what to do when starting with broad goals, one cannot as well tell if he or she is progressing if there is no way to measure progress. A goal being quantifiable is very important for a person to have feedback on his or her progress. It is also the only objective way for one to know if he or she has reached the goal already.

Feedback is necessary in goal attainment. It gives a person a way to determine how his or her efforts are paying off. From that, a person can then identify specific adjustments necessary to better their performance. Feedback is an opportunity to see strengths and weaknesses in relation to environmental or contextual factors. It can also influence a person's motivation and perseverance. Just like goals, feedback must be stated in a specific manner.

Effective goals are also *achievable*. This is what makes wishful thinking and goal setting far different from each other. Goals are meant to be achieved; hence, when one is setting specific and measurable goals, attainability must also be considered. It was revealed through different studies that goals that are too easy to substantial incremental improvement in performance are difficult but achievable goals.

It is natural for a person to work and meet the cognitive challenges handed to them. However, although people seemed to work harder on challenging goals there is a limit to this. If the goals appeared to require performance that one sees to be beyond his or her capacities, it is likely that the desired performance level will not occur. Consequently, the concept of self-efficacy is pivotal in maximizing a person's high performance level.

It is also important to keep in mind that goals that are too difficult will not motivate people. Instead it will discourage them as a too difficult goal is seen as unreasonable. In addition, research also revealed that people have a tendency to resort to dishonesty once they fail to achieve challenging goals.

In setting up goals one must consider his or her abilities, skills and knowledge. Of equal importance is weighing the resources available. These factors will help one develop goals difficult enough to challenge the self without compromising attainability.

The next key characteristic of an effective goal is *relevance.* As mentioned earlier, one of the things that can motivate people is the significance of the goal and its outcomes. Commitment tends to get stronger once the person understands the value of what he or she is working for. Only when the goal is seen as apart of the bigger picture can one fully see its relevance.

Another thing that makes goal effective is being *time-bound.* Goals are something one should be able to reach and complete after a certain period of time. Indeed, there has to be a time limit to make the person not waste any minute of the day. The time-control of having a deadline gives people more motivation and focus on the task completion. It is likely that a person will work harder when the deadline is fast approaching and when a person is ahead of the schedule he or she will slow down and pay more attention to work details.

Deadlines are necessary for goals to be effective. It creates a sense of urgency to make people work harder. However, one must be realistic in setting time limits to complete a goal or task. If the deadline is too tight, it is likely for the quality of job to suffer. Also, instead of motivating people, they might even get frustrated at not being able to stretch their 24 hours in a day.

The time needed for a particular goal is relative. Some goals require three to five years or more to be accomplished; hence, they are called *long-term goals*. Others would need at least half-a year to be completed and these are called *intermediate-term goals.* Lastly, *short-term goals* are those that can be achieved in a week or a month. Among these goals, long-term ones appear to be the most challenging for a person to attain. It is even highly possible for a person to get caught between a highly rewarding long-term goal and the immediate satisfaction of shorter termed goal. The ability to self regulate comes in handy in such situations.

Chapter 6: Goals Are Set, What's Next?

Identifying and setting goals based on the criteria discussed in the previous chapter is just the first step. What follows requires a person to demonstrate his or her ability to self-regulate. When a goal is set, one is recognizing that something must be done or changed and with the sufficient level of commitment, that goal is likely to be attained. Commitment, however, does not do the entire job in goal pursuant. Most of the time, a person needs more than that to succeed. The following are some important considerations that one must keep in mind to be able to successfully achieve a desired future.

Invest Time on Planning. As mentioned earlier, it is important for every goal to be accompanied by specific plans of actions. These plans serve as a step-by-step procedure that will bring a person closer to his or her goals every time. If a person knows exactly what to do to attain a goal, his or her behaviors will always be guided. A plan can be in the form of a schedule enumerating specific tasks that must be accomplished within a specific period of time. As much as goals need to be specific, plans must also be fully detailed.

Planning is the most effective way to avoid wasting effort and resources. According to studies, in contexts where planning is not practiced, 80% of the people's unguided effort produce results less than 20%.

Also, with a plan, it is likely that someone will take into considerations all factors involved in goal attainment. By recognizing different factors that could influence the success of goal achievement, one can easily see which among these factors are critical and need special attention. Planning also allows a person identify all his or her resources available at present and in the future. The planning process also involves the assessment of the impacts of the plan to the self and significant others. Through planning, one also is given the chance to evaluate if all the costs and efforts will all be worth it.

Planning is a cyclical process. It starts with the current situation analysis and ends with a feedback and then it will go back to current situation assessment and so on. Planning includes identifying specific actions and how exactly they will be done.

To make plans more effective, one should keep in mind that simpler and straightforward statements must be used. Also, plans must be flexible. There is no way one could accurately predict the future; hence, it is best to create plans that can adapt to uncontrollable changes. Reviewing and evaluating the plans is also necessary before implementing them. Plan evaluation can be in the form of a simple cost-benefit analysis.

Getting Organized. A sense of structure and order is important for a person pursuing a goal. From setting life goals to implementing them, a sense of organization is needed. Tasks must be distributed between days in a logical fashion. It is not enough to have listed specific activities that are to be performed randomly. There has to be reason why task A is followed by task B, for instance. A sense of organization is also needed for keeping files and records relevant to the accomplishment of goals. Finally, organization through time management is surely a necessity. This will be discussed separately in the succeeding chapters.

Weigh Everything. A person must also learn how to prioritize. It is possible for one to experience some levels of difficulty working on different goals at the same time. Consequently, there has to be some decisions to make. One must understand the reason behind every goal. This will help him or her decide which one should be prioritized for the moment and which can wait.

Keeping an Eye on One's Self. The reason why goals should be measurable is that a person is required to keep track of his or her progress. It is only when everything is recorded that a person can fully judge his or her performance in pursuing a goal. Keeping a record also helps a person identify his or her areas of strengths and areas that must be improved. A person is likely to learn more about themselves in the process and they can have a better sense of self-worth after every performance assessment.

It is also important for a person to be brutally honest in assessing the self. Facts must be faced in accordance with the reality that is happening. Sugarcoating issues and concerns will not help a person reach his or her desired destination.

Discipline One's Self. Keeping up with plans might be more challenging than expected. Indeed, some goal-oriented tasks are rather difficult to complete. At times like this, a person may resort to strategies that could strictly guide the behavior modification process. Implementing rewards and punishments can be used to strengthen one's commitment to stay on track by completing goal-directed tasks and performing desired behaviors.

For instance, one can treat themselves with a special meal in a fine dining restaurant if they were able to clear the weekly tasks they had planned. It is also possible for one to punish him or her self by removing desirable stimulus. For example, a student who is aiming at a 0.6 increase in her GPA failed two of her examination. She then will punish herself by surrendering her cellphone, Ipad and laptop to her parents for them to keep for a day or two. Having undesirable consequences for every task completion failure can surely make a person more determined to stick with the plan and exert more effort.

The value of rewards and the gravity of punishments, however, must be well thought out. It should be proportion to the difficulty of the tasks completed. Small rewards are fitting for minor achievements. In the same manner, minor punishments must be appropriate for trivial mistakes or failures.

Gather Support. In striving for a goal, asking for other people's help is never wrong. Indeed, even if the goals are generally personal, one can still ask his or her family and friends for support. One should start by informing other people about his or her goals. Since goals are generally desirable future outcomes, it is of high probability that other people will be supportive of one's goals. It is likely for a person striving to meet goal to be more motivated if the people around him or her offer encouragement and support.

Consider Setbacks as Learning Experience. In reality, goal attainment is not as simple as establishing goals and plans, implementing them and then living happily ever after. There are going to be tough times when none of what's written in the plans is working well. Hindrances can always get in the way and ruin one's drive or determination. Problems will rise to challenge a person further.

Indeed, setbacks are common in goal attainment and it is something one must expect. Nevertheless, there are more important factors to consider other than the problems, setbacks and hindrances- that is, how a person sees these things. If one can easily be disheartened by failures, achieving goals can be difficult. Instead of seeing setback as a pulling factor, one must learn to interpret it as a pushing factor. Failure brings learning and learning makes one think and act better.

Negative thoughts have no place in the goal attainment process. Considering possible obstacles is good but keeping the negativities in mind is bad. Negative thoughts are hindrances in themselves. A person cannot perform his or her best when undesirable fears and thoughts nest in his or her mind. Indeed, a positive kind of mind-set is the one that can help a person achieve goals.

Enjoy. Motivation plays a pivotal role in goal setting and implementation. Hence, it is necessary for one to keep his or her motivation alive until the goal is reached. One way to keep one's motivation where it should be is to include enjoyable activities in the plan. The process of striving for goals does not need to be dull and too rigid. A person knows him or herself best; hence, he or she should incorporate activities that he or she finds enjoyable in the action plan. Of course, this must not get in the way of the goal attainment plans.

For instance, a person who aims at losing 10 lbs of body weight for an X period of time need not to spend all their time in the gym. It is possible to do different activities in different places like swimming in the nearby beach, or jogging around the neighborhood. One could also lose weight by taking up dancing classes and learning new sports. There are several ways one can accomplish specific tasks. One only needs a little bit of creativity to see these various options.

Complete the Process. One must finish what he or she started. Once the goal implementation starts to roll, it is necessary for one to keep it rolling until the desired outcome is reached. Indeed, fleeting commitment will never work on successful goal achievement.

Achieving goals is really hard work. Hence, determination, self-efficacy, motivation and strong commitment are all necessary for one to reach the desired outcome. Nevertheless, the benefits of goal setting are worthy enough for the amount of efforts necessary. Goals can really be beneficial but there are instances where setting goals can be dysfunctional. This includes rare occasions where people become demoralized by giving themselves goals in an inappropriate time and place. Just like any other tool for progress, goals setting can be used in a dysfunctional manner that causes more troubles than desirable outcomes.

Chapter 7: Introduction To Time Management

1440 minutes in a day, 7 days in a week and 365 days in an entire year. Time is indeed a finite resource. Money cannot extend time. It is, perhaps, the only resource given equally to people, rich or poor. Indeed, one cannot get more time as it is fixed. This is the reason why time is gold. A wasted period of time cannot be recycled; once it's gone, it *is* gone.

People usually complain about having so much to do with too little time. Several people have experienced a point in their life where they wished there was more than 24 hours in a day. Most people typically see the finite nature of time as a limiting factor. Nevertheless, if seen from a different angle, the fixed amount of time available can actually be advantageous to people. With a constant number of hours in a day, one need not think about how much time is available. One only needs to focus on how much work can be done in a day. Even if one cannot control the length of time, one can definitely have the power to control how to use every precious minute of it.

People can easily be overwhelmed by the several aspects of their lives that are demanding time from them. Hence, they always feel like they are out of control of their own time. In reality, however, people do have control of their use of time. Time just needs to be managed and by doing so, one can make the most out of it.

What is Time Management?

The use of time management as a term is very common to people. Several seminars or books on time management are available for the public. Despite the commonality of the term use, however, a universal definition is still out of existence.

There are several ways that time both laymen and experts describe management. The ability to take control over time, spontaneity, flexibility and balance are some just some of these ways.

Time management is referred to by some as a process enabling a person to effectively accomplish his or her goals and tasks. It is also seen as a habit that can be cultivated by practice and determination. Time management is also seen as the ability to prioritize and respect such priorities. Some state that time management is a process through which a person gains control over time and the content of the activities scheduled.

There is also a debate on what particular behavior and skills are necessary for effective time management. Some suggests principles to follow such as self-awareness, setting goals, establishing priorities, structuring time and allotting time for both activities and relaxation. More recent behavioral suggestions for effective management of time include making lists, setting goals, organizing tasks, and compartmenting tasks into smaller chunks.

Despite the lack of universal definition and principles of time management, several studies attest its benefits to people. Juggling workloads from the different aspects of human life can be less overwhelming and frustrating with the proper implementation of an active time management system. Whether you are a student, corporate employee, parent, freelance worker or an artist, being able to accomplish tasks accordingly and timely will definitely help you live a better life.

Chapter 8: Why Spend Time Managing Time?

As a limited resource, time really needs to be utilized wisely. People cannot live forever and they cannot buy or store time for emergency needs. Time will always be fixed, limited and non-renewable. While time is limited, people's need for it seems to grow as time passes by. People need time to accomplish several life activities, goals and pre-occupations. Thus, it always appears to majority of the people that there is not enough time.

Managing time can make a person accomplish more with lesser effort wasted. Indeed, efficiency is what time management brings to a person's life. Efficiency leads to enhanced productivity and this opens up more time that one can use for other significant activities.

With time management one is also able to avoid distractions by prioritizing only those things that of at most significance for goal realization. Since time is limited, key actions will be given time allotment first while insignificant activities can be eliminated from the daily schedule.

A person overwhelmed by the piles of workloads usually end up just staring blankly at nothingness. The feeling of powerlessness consumes the person, as he or she cannot even imagine how to squeeze in all the work that has to be done with the limited time he or she has. Such negative thoughts and emotions can be reduced and later on eliminated by effective time management. Indeed, being able to plan specific tasks for every hour of the day can empower a person. In turn, this feeling of empowerment can make a person play an active role in achieving life goals.

Chapter 9: How Not To Waste Time

It All Starts with a Goal in Mind

Goal setting and implementation are central to time management. The very reason why one is working on time management is to be able to successfully accomplish daily tasks pivotal to the desired future outcome. Specific goals can help a person take control of the wheel of his or her life. The person can decide the routes to take and eliminate unnecessary detours. In the same manner, time management provides one with a sense of control over how he or she can maximize the limited hours of the day.

Let Go of What Cannot be Controlled

People complain a lot about having not enough time to finish their tasks for the day. Then they have a habit of spending time wishing that the universe would suddenly add more hours in a day. Rarely do these people realize that by constantly complaining and thinking about how to make days longer than 24-hours, they are actually wasting time. Indeed, every single minute counts.

Worrying is also a waste of time. When the tasks to be accomplished appeared too overwhelming, people usually spend more time worrying about not being able to finish on time than they do working on the project. People also tend to worry about things they cannot control. These worries assault a person's self-efficacy and determination. The problem with worrying is that it usually lingers in a person's mind, making him or her unproductive for a certain period of time.

Invest in Planning

A day should be planned for. If it is not, you will definitely waste time as you execute your daily activities. Thinking and making a detailed action plan on a daily basis can be considered by others as a waste of time. These people would rather jump into mountains of work immediately and start attending to tasks that they get a hold of first. In actuality, having a plan and organization before starting a project can help one manage time better. Planning ahead gives one a sense of direction.

If you allot time to think through the project at hand prior to its implementation, you will foresee possible problems that might arise. Given that, you can prepare for such troubles. Planning efforts also includes gathering materials, compiling records necessary and preparing other resources needed to complete the tasks of the day. This kind of preparedness and organization will save you time by eliminating the chances of not being able to start anything because of the unavailability of resources or materials.

Preparation is indeed valuable. You can be more productive just by allotting even a small portion of your time to plan ahead.

One Task at a Time

For some, doing several things at the same time works just fine, or so it seems. In everyday life, multitasking takes place in several occasions. Parents are typically depicted as being as busy as bees in the mornings, preparing breakfast while helping their children get ready and at the same time responding to their partner's queries about where their keys are.

Although it generally appears fine, research has revealed that multitasking is actually a waste of time. Performing two tasks at the same time is said to be a highly ineffective manner of getting things done. According to studies, the brain slows down as it switches from varying memory experience and activating different sets of skills. Hence, one is wasting time attending to different tasks all at once.

Perhaps, multitasking cannot be entirely avoided, as it can be helpful in certain circumstances. However, when the task is difficult or is crucial for one's goals, it is best to avoid multitasking. As studies suggest, working on one task at a time is more effective and productive.

Positive Vibes

While working on a very demanding project, the last thing you need is to be surrounded by people who are negative thinkers. Other people can easily influence your mindset and there lies the danger of spending time with pessimists. You are likely to be influenced by their undesirable thoughts, worries and feelings. Instead of being in the company of these kinds of people, you should find a place where you can cultivate a positive mindset. Finding a crowd of enthusiastic and productive individuals can also help.

Overdoing something is Never Fruitful

Taking breaks is necessary for you to be more productive. It is natural for a person to experience a dramatic decline in their concentration and energy after hours of working. This is the sign that the brain and body need a refresher. Having breaks in between long hours of work gives you a refreshed feeling, revitalized energy and regained focus. Some people consider breaks as waste of time so they always opt not to take even a five-minute rest. Nevertheless, such an inclination does not make them more productive. People who do not take breaks usually get caught reading the same paragraph over and over again and end up not understanding any of what it states. It is also common for them to experience making mistakes with even the simplest task, like printing report pages. Indeed, without breaks, your performance suffers.

Breaks are best implemented in a short yet frequent manner. If you are allowed to have a 15-minute coffee break in a day, you can spend it as three five-minute breaks. That way, you can have more chances to renew your focus and energy.

Chapter 10: The Do's: Cultivating Time Management Skills

The ability to effectively manage time is not an innate characteristic. It is something you can develop over time. Anyone can cultivate certain habits to help maximize every minute of the day. Time management requires effort, commitment and self-belief; nevertheless, the outcome will surely outweigh the costs.

Waking up early is one habit a person could start cultivating. You will be surprised how much you can accomplish if you start the day early. Most people are highly productive during the first hours in the morning. This must be taken advantage of. Also, if there are big projects or tasks to be accomplished the following day, you should wake up earlier than normal. By doing so, you are stretching your available time in preparation for the big task.

Keeping healthy is also necessary. Some people mistakenly assume that while working with a strict time management system, skipping meals or breaks is typical. This, however, is a maladaptive belief. To be able to keep up with a tight schedule, a person actually needs to be at his or her best physically and emotionally. Hence, you should make a habit of eating healthy food.

Instead of eating big full meals, you may consider small but rather frequent meals. A big meal can indeed make you full but you might feel lethargic. This makes thinking and moving slower; hence, you become less productive. A balanced diet is also important. Eating junk foods and drinking sodas should be avoided. Keeping yourself healthy is, perhaps, the best way for you to ensure your effectiveness at work.

In addition to keeping a healthy diet, you must also allot time to exercise. Keep in mind that exercising not only keeps you physically healthy, it also improves your mental health. Exercising can help stimulate and energize the brain, making you more productive.

It is best for you to include at least 20 minutes of exercise time in your daily schedule. Nevertheless, most people claim that they do not have the luxury of time to even do some stretching. If it is really impossible for you to give exercising some time, you must start incorporating some physical activity to your daily routine. For instance, if tasks usually done while sitting can be performed while standing, then you should opt for the latter. Studies reveal that sitting for long hours can actually shorten one's life. You can also use the stairs instead of the elevator. If possible, you should walk to work instead of driving or taking a cab. A couple of minutes spent lifting hand weights or doing some crunches at home can be good enough if done regularly. Even small increments of physical activity can help improve one's physical and mental health.

Part of keeping healthy is getting enough sleep. An insufficient amount of sleep can make you move and think slower. Also, you become irritable and grumpy when deprived of sleep. None of these behaviors will help you perform your best to reach a goal.

Learn How to Say No

With a time management system, you assign significant activities that must be accomplished within the specified time frame. Hence, it can be expected your day is well planned. However, it is highly possible for you to encounter factors that can potentially disrupt your schedule. Indeed, it is important for your plan to be flexible but this is for the purpose of entertaining crucial matters only and not petty things. Thus, you should learn how to say "No" in the most polite manner to a dinner invite, for instance. Sticking to the schedule is important for you to achieve your goals.

In relation to saying "No" to unplanned events, you should also learn to take an active control of social interactions while working. Social encounters can hinder a person from sticking to his or her plans for the day. For instance, an intended short conversation can become too lengthy if the person is not active in controlling his or her interactions with others. However, you must not totally avoid interactions just to be able to have more work hours. A smooth flowing working relationship with co-workers is as significant for your productivity. Consequently, you may consider having a chat with co-workers first thing in the morning while everyone is still setting up. Also, small talk during lunch breaks is a good way to display friendliness even in the midst of a very busy day.

Setting Time for Distracting Thoughts

Perhaps it is a common experience among people to suddenly be visited by unnecessary random thoughts while in the middle of a task. It can be about anything, a new recipe one wanted to try, or a sudden idea on how to spend holidays or even the kind of hairstyle that a person wants to try. The best way to deal with such disturbing thoughts is to acknowledge them. Writing down the random thought can make letting go of it rather easy.

Another technique to keep a distracting thought or even worrying ideas from your mind is to set a time of the day when you will deal with nothing but the said thoughts and worries. For instance, you can set 5:00 to 5:20 in the afternoon as your "worry time". So, whenever a distracting thought suddenly popped, you should literally instruct yourself to stop thinking about it and wait until the worry time comes.

Keeping an Effective Time Management System: Planning the Day

Once the goals are set and the plans have been evaluated, you can start making further plans by scheduling daily activities. A planner is necessary for you to be guided while you work on your daily tasks.

In planning the daily activities, you should start with enumerating all the actions, tasks or activities that you need to accomplish. There is really no need to rank them at this stage. The goal of this step is to identify all the tasks without missing anything.

Afterwards, you should pick the top activities that are crucial. These tasks can be identified by asking yourself about how urgent each task is and the possible consequences if it is not done immediately. Indeed, this step is where you create a hierarchy among the listed tasks. Listed activities that are unnecessary must be eliminated from the list.

Once the tasks are clustered, the next step is allotting time slots for each activity, starting with the priority clusters. The time frame must be realistic and very specific. Next is to evaluate the schedule done and make adjustments if necessary. To be prepared for any unforeseen factors that would make the schedule impossible, you must have a back up schedule prepared. This, however, must only be utilized once the first schedule of activities is prevented from working out well.

What's left is the implementation of the plans. This, however, is a crucial part. You must have the determination, commitment, motivation and physical and mental energy to successfully carry out all the tasks for the day without compromising quality.

Conclusion

Thank you again for purchasing this book!

I hope this book was able to help you understand what makes goal setting and time management effective.

The next step is to apply the specific guidelines mentioned in pursuit of your personal or professional life goals. You may also share the knowledge learned from this book to your family and friends to help them perform better in achieving their desired future.

Thank you and good luck!